Mammals of Canada

Einstein Sisters

KidsWorld

Bison

The bison is the **largest** land mammal in **Canada**. A bison can weigh almost as much as a small car.

Bison use their heads to **plow through** deep snow.

A male bison is called **a bull.** The female is called a cow. A baby **bison** is called a **calf.**

The **bison** has a very **strong neck.** The **hump** between its shoulders is **made of muscle.**

Mountain Goat

A male goat is **called a billy.** The **female** is called a nanny. A baby goat is called a **kid.**

Each **hoof** has a **soft, rubbery** pad on the **bottom** to **help** the mountain goat's feet **grip** rocks.

You can tell how **old a mountain goat** is by counting the **rings on its horns.**

The mountain goat's woolly, white coat keeps it warm high in the mountains. The coat has two layers—the long hairs on top cover a short, thick undercoat.

Humpbacks like to **jump** out of the water. That is called "**breaching.**" They also like to **slap** their **long flippers** on the **water.**

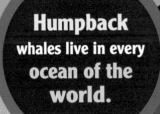

Humpback whales live in every **ocean of the world.**

A male whale is called a bull. The **female** is called a cow. A baby whale is called **a calf.**

Humpback Whale

These whales **sing long, complicated songs.** They use these songs to **talk to** other **humpbacks.**

A male deer is called a buck. The female is called a doe. A baby deer is called **a fawn.**

White-tailed Deer

The **white-tailed deer** is the most common **large mammal** in **Canada.**

The deer's tail is white underneath. When a deer **senses danger**, it raises its tail and shows the white patch. This **tells other deer** to run away to a **safe place.**

A **doe** leaves her fawn alone for many hours each day. The fawn's spots help it **hide from predators.**

A male bear
is called **a boar.**
The female is called a sow.
A baby bear is called
a cub.

Bears are very strong and unpredictable. You should always be very cautious around bears.

Even though black bears look slow and clumsy, they can run very fast.

Black bears hibernate, which means they sleep all winter.

Black Bear

Moose

The **moose** is the **largest** member of the **deer** family. It is **taller** than a horse.

A male moose is called a bull. The female is called a cow. A baby moose is called **a calf.**

Moose are good swimmers. They can stay underwater for **up to 1 minute.**

Only male moose have **antlers.** The antlers are **wide** and flattened.

Caribou are a kind of deer. They live in the northern parts of each province and in the Arctic.

Caribou

A **male** caribou is called a bull. The **female** is called a cow. A baby caribou is called **a calf.**

Both male and female caribou **grow antlers.** The male's antlers are **bigger** than the female's.

Caribou live in large herds. They **migrate north** in spring and **return south** in winter. They travel more than **2500 kilometres every year.**

Orcas live in every ocean of the **world.**

Orca

A male orca is called a bull. The female is **called a cow.** A baby orca is **called a calf.**

The male orca has a tall, triangular fin on his back. The female's fin is shorter **and curved.**

The **oldest known orca** in the world is about **103 years old.** Scientists call her **"Granny."**

Orcas are **sometimes** called "killer whales." The orca is the **largest** member of the **dolphin family.**

Wolverine

The **wolverine** is the **largest** member of the weasel family. It lives mostly in **northern Canada.**

Some people call the **wolverine** "skunk bear" because it is almost as **stinky** as a skunk.

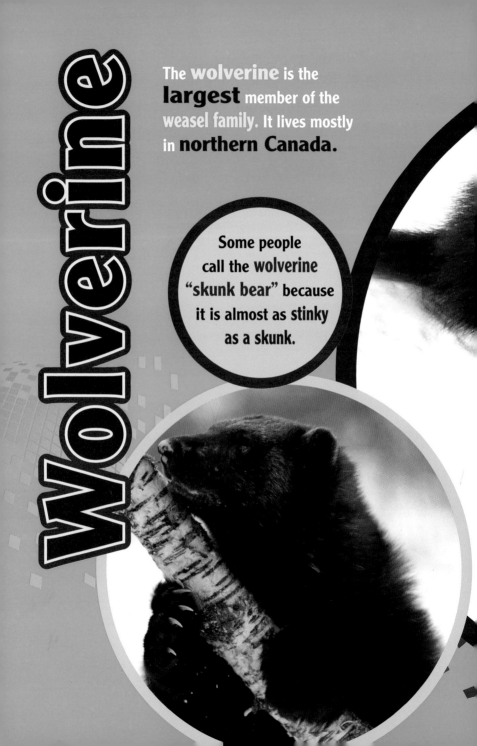

Wolverines prefer to **eat dead animals** instead of hunting for their **own food**. They will even **scare bears** away and **steal their food**.

Wolverines have **big, furry paws** that keep them from **sinking** into the snow. Their **thick fur** keeps them warm **in winter**.

Otters like to play. They like to slide down snowbanks or muddy riverbanks.

Northern River Otter

Otters always **live near water.** They eat mostly fish. They also eat **frogs, insects and** shellfish.

An otter can **stay underwater** for **8 minutes.** It can close its **nostrils and ears** so **no water gets in.**

Otters have two layers of fur. The thick **outer fur is waterproof.** The soft inner layer of fur keeps the **otter warm.**

Elk

Only male elk have antlers. The antlers start growing in spring and **fall off** in the winter. While growing, they have a **fuzzy covering** called "velvet."

Elk are also called "wapiti." They are related to deer.

A **male** elk is called a **bull**. The **female** is called a **cow**. A baby elk is called a **calf**.

In the late summer and fall, male elk "bugle" to attract females.

A male porpoise is called **a bull.**
The female is called a cow.
A baby porpoise
is called **a**
calf.

The **harbour porpoise** is one of the **smallest marine mammals.** Harbour porpoises swim in **shallow waters** along our **coastlines.**

This **porpoise** makes a sneezing sound when it **surfaces.** Some people call it **"puffing porpoise."**

Harbour Porpoise

The harbour porpoise eats small **fish and squid.** It sucks its prey into its mouth and **swallows it whole.**

A raccoon can **grow** as big as a **medium-sized dog.**

A **male** raccoon is called a boar. The **female** is called a sow. A baby raccoon is called **a kit.**

Raccoon

Raccoons have very **sensitive paws.** They often **examine** their food in water. The water makes the **skin** on their paws softer, so they can feel things **better.**

Raccoons are **active** mostly at night. They **live** in **forests** and in **cities,** where they like to steal food from **garbage cans.**

Bighorn sheep live in **herds** with up to **100** members.

Bighorn Sheep

Bighorn rams have contests to win females. The males **run** toward each other and **smash** their heads together. The **strongest one** gets to mate with **the ewes.**

A **baby** bighorn sheep is called a **lamb.**

Male bighorn
sheep are called **rams**.
They have **long, curled horns**.
Females are called **ewes**
and have **shorter horns**
that **don't curl**.

Weasels are fierce hunters. They usually eat mice, insects and small birds, but they sometimes catch **bigger prey** such as **rabbits or chickens.**

A weasel stays warm in winter by **curling into a ball.**

Instead of **walking** or running, weasels make a series of **jumps.**

Short-tailed Weasel

In winter, the **short-tailed** weasel is completely white, except for a **black tail tip.**

Porcupine

A porcupine has **soft hair,** but on its back, sides and tail, the hair is mixed with **sharp quills.** It has about **30,000 quills.**

A male porcupine is called a **boar.** The female is called **a sow.** A baby porcupine is called a porcupette.

Porcupines can't **shoot** their **quills** at attackers. The quills **come out** easily when **touched.**

Porcupines like to **climb trees.** They eat leaves, twigs and bark. **They love salt.**

The grey wolf is the **largest** member of the dog family.

Wolves and **coyotes** look alike, but wolves are bigger. Wolves also have a **wider** snout, **bigger feet** and **longer legs** than coyotes do.

Wolf pups have **blue eyes** when they are born. Their eyes **change colour** after a few months. Most wolves have **yellow eyes.**

Wolves live in groups called packs. Packs usually have about 10 members.

Grey Wolf

A cougar
looks like a house cat,
but it is about the size of an
adult human. The cougar
is also called "puma" or
"mountain lion."

Cougar

Cougars have very **powerful** legs. They can **jump** as high as the **roof** of a house.

Cougars are good swimmers, but they **don't** like water.

The cougar is the **largest** cat that purrs.

Muskrat

Muskrats always live near water. They make houses from cattails and rushes. Sometimes they dig burrows in the banks of rivers and lakes.

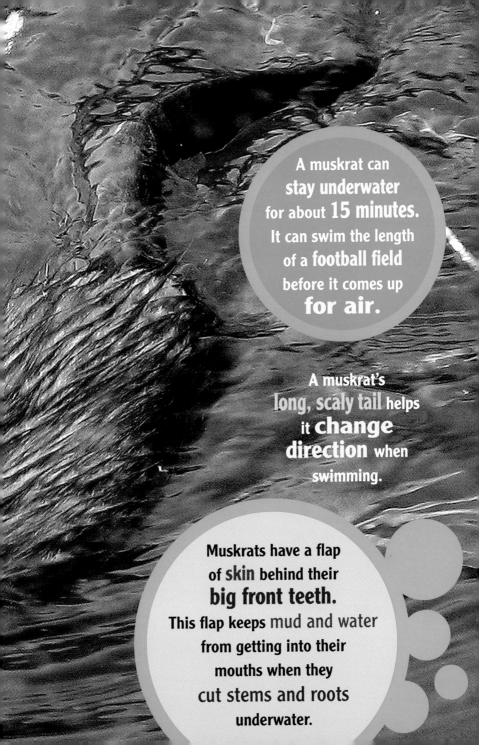

A muskrat can **stay underwater** for about **15 minutes.** It can swim the length of a **football field** before it comes up **for air.**

A muskrat's **long, scaly tail** helps it **change direction** when swimming.

Muskrats have a flap of **skin** behind their **big front teeth.** This flap keeps mud and water from getting into their mouths when they **cut stems and roots** underwater.

Coyote

Coyotes will eat almost anything. They hunt for rabbits, mice, frogs and insects, but they also eat dead animals and garbage.

The coyote is a member of the dog family. It lives almost everywhere in Canada, even in cities.

Coyotes communicate with barks, yips and howls. Sometimes many coyotes "sing" together in a chorus.

Coyotes often live in family groups called **packs.** A pair of coyotes mates for life.

Beaver

The beaver uses its **large,** paddle-shaped tail to steer as it swims. It can close its ears and nose when it swims underwater.

The beaver is **Canada's** national symbol. Beavers cut down small trees to **build dams** and **make ponds.**

A beaver's front teeth never stop growing. It has to **chew** on tree **trunks and branches** to keep its teeth from getting **too long.**

A beaver's house is called a "lodge." It is made from sticks and **small tree trunks.** The entrance is under water.

A male skunk is called a boar. The female is called a sow. A baby skunk is called **a kit.**

If a skunk is angry or afraid, it will shoot a stinky spray at its attacker. Skunk spray smells awful but it **doesn't hurt.**

A skunk is about the **same size** as a cat.

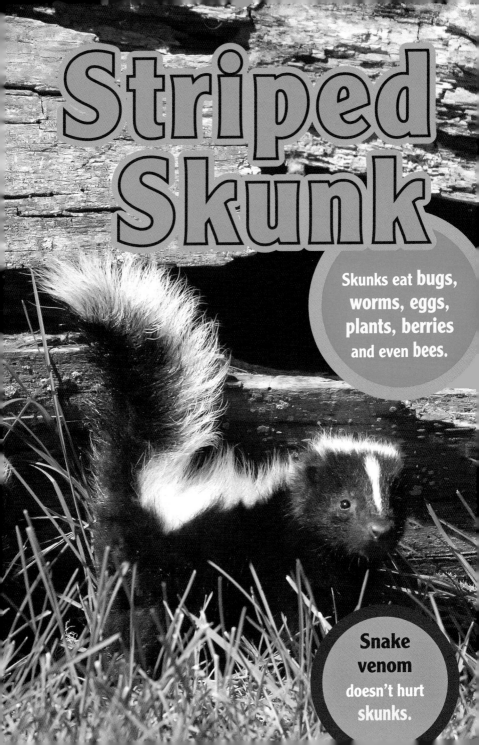

Striped Skunk

Skunks eat **bugs, worms, eggs, plants, berries** and even **bees.**

Snake **venom** doesn't hurt skunks.

Eastern cottontails are a kind of rabbit. They are named for their white, fluffy tails.

Rabbits **don't change colour** in the winter like **hares** do. Their **fur** stays brown or grey all year-round.

Baby rabbits don't have any fur when they are **born.** They are completely helpless and **can't hop** around.

Eastern Cottontail

A male rabbit is called a buck. The female is called a doe. A baby rabbit is called a bunny or a kit.

Little Brown Bat

A little brown bat **weighs** about as much as a **loonie or a toonie.** It is as long as an **adult's hand** is wide.

Bats **live in** groups called **colonies.** A colony can have **thousands** of bats.

To find food, a bat **sends out** a **high-frequency sound** that bounces off objects. The **echo** that returns tells the bat where the prey is. This is called **"echolocation."**

Bats **hunt** at **night**. They eat while they are **flying**. A bat can eat up to **1000 insects** in a night.

Chipmunks **sleep during winter,** but squirrels are active all **year-round.**

Least Chipmunk

The least chipmunk is the smallest chipmunk in Canada. Its tail is about as **long as its body.**

Least chipmunks mostly eat **seeds and nuts.** They **carry food** in cheek **pouches** so they can eat it later or **store it for winter.**

Chipmunks live in **holes in trees** or in **burrows** underground. Some make nests in tree **branches.**

Lynx

A lynx can't run very fast so it sneaks up on its prey. Lynxes eat rabbits and other small animals.

Lynxes like to hunt and travel alone. They hunt at night and can see well in the dark.

The lynx's large, furry paws act like snowshoes. When the lynx walks, its toes spread out so it doesn't sink in the snow.

Lynx kittens stay with their mother for about a year. She teaches them to hunt.

The walrus lives in the far north. Its body has a thick layer of fat called "blubber." It keeps the walrus warm in the cold water.

A walrus **can stay underwater** for **20 minutes.** It dives to the **bottom** of the ocean to look for **clams,** its favourite food.

Walrus

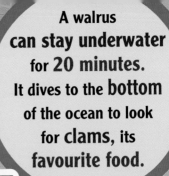

A **male** walrus is called **a bull.** The **female** is called a cow. A baby walrus is called **a calf.**

Walruses use their **tusks** to help pull their heavy bodies out of the water onto the ice. They also use their tusks to chop breathing holes in the ice.

A male hare is called a **buck**. The female is called a doe. A baby hare is called **a leveret.**

Snowshoe hares are **brown** in summer and **white** in winter. The tips of their ears are **always black.**

Baby snowshoe hares **have fur** and can **hop around** as soon as they are **born.**

The hare's big back feet are like snowshoes. They have thick, stiff fur and toes that spread out to help the hare move over snow.

Showshoe Hare

Red Squirrel

Red squirrels spend most of their time looking for food. They mostly eat the seeds of pine and spruce trees.

Red squirrels are very noisy. They even chirp when they are alone.

Squirrels store spruce and pine cones in holes in trees and other places. One squirrel can **store** as many as **14,000 cones in a year.**

A red squirrel gets new fur on its body twice a year. Once a year, it **regrows** all the **fur on its tail.**

Bobcat

Bobcats are fierce hunters. They can kill prey much bigger than themselves, but they usually eat rabbits, mice and squirrels.

A bobcat is about twice the size of a house cat.

The bobcat is the most common wildcat in North America. It is named for its short, bobbed tail.

A baby bobcat is called a kitten.

The **male fox** is called **a dog.** The female is called a vixen. A baby fox is called a pup, a cub or a kit.

Foxes hunt mostly **at night.** They **can see** really well **in the dark.**

Foxes eat small animals such as **mice and rabbits.** They catch them by **jumping** high in the air and landing on top of their **prey.**

Foxes can climb trees. Sometimes they like to **sit** on low branches.

Red Fox

~y KidsWorld Books

~t printed in 2015 10 9 8 7 6 5 4 3 2 1

Printed in China

The Publisher: KidsWorld Books

Library and Archives Canada Cataloguing in Publication

Mammals of Canada / Einstein Sisters.

ISBN 978-0-9940069-3-6 (pbk.)

1. Mammals—Canada—Juvenile literature. I. Einstein Sisters, author

QL721.M2 2015   j599.0971   C2015-901209-0

Cover Images: Front cover: cougar, MikeLane45/Thinkstock. *Back cover:* humpback whale, Jim Tierney/Thinkstock; bison, dmbaker/Thinkstock; little brown bat, Geoff Kuchera/Thinkstock.

Background Graphics: abstract background, Maryna Borysevych/Thinkstock, 9, 21, 29, 51; pixels, Misko Kordic/Thinkstock, 2, 4, 13, 16, 18, 22, 25, 27, 30, 32, 35, 37, 40, 42, 47, 48, 52, 58, 62.

Photo Credits: Ken Balcomb, 25; Seattle Support Group/Photos.com, 4. *From Flickr:* Brian Gratwicke, 50; Denali National Park and Preserve, 14–15; Keith Shannon, U.S. Forestry and Wildlife Service, 48; Steve Hersey, 42–43; U.S. Forestry and Wildlife Service, 30b. *From Thinkstock:* Anthony Rix, 32–33; Comstock Images, 44; Daniel Loiselle, 20–21; Dean_Fikar, 42; dmbaker, 2–3; edevansuk, 29b; Evgeniya Lazareva, 16; exies, 51; gatito33, 31; Genfirstlight, 62; Geoff Kuchera, 35, 41, 48–49, 60–61; Guy Sagi, 8; Jim Tierney, 6–7; Ihar Byshniou, 63; jamenpercy, 18; jcrader, 5; John Pitcher, 34; johnrandallaves, 23; Jupiterimages, 32, 52, 55; Lightwriter1949, 9; Lynn Bystrom, 11, 45; MathildeMenard, 18–19; MikeLane45, 36, 53; miroloschkin, 58; PaulReevesPhotography, 46; photobirder, 13; photographybyJHWilliams, 12; Purestock, 22; Robert Blanchard, 27; RONSAN4D, 56; TanyaNozawa, 26; Tom Brakefield, 10, 15; Tom Tietz, 37, 40; USO, 38; Vladimir Chernyanskiy, 29a; Yuqun Cao, 30a; zanskar, 54. *From Wikipedia:* AVampireTear, 24; Connormah, 58–59; D. Gordon E. Robertson, 38–39, 56–57; J Schmidt, 2; public domain, 17; Steve Hillebrand, U.S. Forestry and Wildlife Service, 28; The High Fin Sperm Whale, 47.

We acknowledge the financial support of the Government of Canada through the Canada Book Fund (CBF) for our publishing activities.

 Canadian Patrimoine
Heritage canadien

PC: 30